19

OUR PLACES OF WORSHIP

Sikhism

Honor Head

WAYLAND

First published in 2009
by Wayland

Copyright © Wayland 2009

Wayland
338 Euston Road
London NW1 3BH

Wayland Australia
Level 17/207 Kent Street
Sydney NSW 2000

Commissioning editor: Jennifer Sanderson
Editor: Jean Coppendale
Designer: Paul Manning
Consultant: Kanwaljit Singh, Education Inspector
    and Consultant; Deputy Director of Education
    for Network of Sikh Organisations (NSO);
    Chair, British Sikh Education Council

British Library Cataloguing in Publication Data
Head, Honor.
Sikhism. — (Our places of worship)
1. Temples, Sikh—Juvenile literature.
2. Public worship—Sikhism—Juvenile literature.
3. Sikhism—Juvenile literature.
I. Title II. Series
294.6'35-dc22

ISBN 978 0 7502 4928 7

Picture credits

l = left r = right t = top b= bottom
Cover, 4, 5, 6, 7, 10b, 11, 12, 13t, 14, 15, 16, 18, 19t, 20r, 21, 23: Discovery Media/Our Places of
Worship; 8l: G.W. Images/ Ultimathule/ Shutterstock; 8r: Christine Osborne/Alamy; 10t: World Religions
Photo Library/Alamy; 13: World Religions Photo Library/Alamy/ Alamy; 17t: Gerry Walden/Alamy;
17b: Ngo Thye Aun/ Shutterstock; 19b: Reuters/Corbis; 20l: Ajmone Tristana/Shutterstock;
22: Superstock; 24, 25: Ark Religion.com/Alamy; 26: Ian Goodrick/ Alamy; 27t: Tom Pietrasik/Corbis;
27b: Munish Sharma/Corbis; 28: Tibor Bognar/Corbis; 29t: Amit Bhargara/Corbis; 29b: Christine
Osborne/Corbis.

Printed in China

Wayland is a division of Hachette Children's Books,
an Hachette UK company.
www.hachette.co.uk

This book can be used in conjunction with the
interactive CD-Rom, *Our Places of Worship*. To do
this, look for ⊙ and the file path. For example,
material on Sikh gurdwaras can be found on
⊙ Sikhism/Worship/Worship at the Gurdwara.
From the main menu of the whiteboard, click on
'Sikhism', then 'Worship' and then 'Worship
at the Gurdwara'.

To see a sample from the CD-Rom, log on to
www.waylandbooks.co.uk

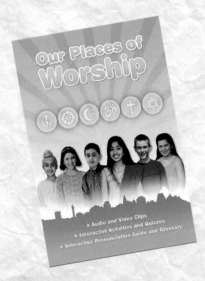

Our Places of Worship
Single user licence: ISBN 978 0 7502 5303 1
School library service licence: ISBN 978 0 7502 5532 5
Site user licence ISBN 978 0 7502 5533 2

Contents

Words appearing in
bold, like this, can be
found in the Glossary
on page 30.

What is a gurdwara?

A gurdwara is a special place where **Sikhs** meet and worship together. People can go to the gurdwara to worship at any time and on any day. Some Sikhs visit it twice a day, once in the morning and again in the evening. People from all religions are welcome at the gurdwara.

▶ Most people go to the gurdwara at weekends, when they do not have to work and they can worship together with their family.

4

Sikhism/Worship/Worship at the Gurdwara

Gurdwaras can look very different from the outside. This gurdwara used to be a house.

This large gurdwara is in Birmingham, England. Inside there are five prayer halls.

Outside a gurdwara

An orange flag is flown outside all gurdwaras so that people will know they are Sikh places of worship. The flag is called the Nishan Sahib (see page 20). The black symbol on the flag is called the Khanda. Some gurdwaras have golden domes and tall towers.

Community centre

A gurdwara is not only a place of worship but it is also a community centre. People can go there to study, to eat, to meet and talk about different things and, if necessary, to sleep. There are no chairs in the gurdwara. Everyone sits on the floor as a sign that all people are equal.

WHAT DO YOU THINK?

Why do you think it is important to have a special place to worship?

Why do you think sitting on the floor shows all people are equal?

Welcome to the gurdwara

When people enter the gurdwara, they take off their shoes. This is a sign of **respect** and it also keeps the gurdwara clean. All gurdwaras have a prayer hall where people pray. Before people go into the prayer hall, they cover their heads. This shows respect for God and for the **Guru Granth Sahib** – the Sikh holy scripture (see pages 10-11). In some countries people wash their feet, too.

◀ Inside the gurdwara is a place where worshippers can leave their shoes.

▶ Some people also like to wash their hands before they enter the prayer hall.

▲ Prayer halls usually have a carpet, which is covered with white sheets to help keep it clean.

Prayer halls

Some gurdwaras have more than one prayer hall. This hall can be big or small. In most gurdwaras the prayer hall is bright and colourful to show that Sikhs are happy when they worship God.

Sitting down

Sometimes men sit on the floor on one side of the prayer hall and women sit on the other side. They sit separately so that they can concentrate on their prayers and worship. In other countries families sit and worship together. Everyone faces the Guru Granth Sahib. Those people who cannot sit on the floor can sit on chairs at the back of the hall.

The Guru Granth Sahib

▶ The word **Guru** means 'teacher' and the Guru Granth Sahib teaches Sikhs how to behave.

7

Preparing for prayer

When Sikhs go into the prayer hall, they first go up to the Guru Granth Sahib and bow and touch the floor with their head as a sign of respect. Next, they leave **donations** of food, flowers or money. The food is shared out later and the money is used to look after the gurdwara. Then the worshippers sit on the floor ready for prayer.

▲ After bowing to the Guru Granth Sahib, Sikhs leave gifts of food, flowers and money.

GURU GOBIND SINGH

The Sikh religion was developed by ten Gurus, or holy men. The tenth Guru was called Gobind Singh who died in 1708. He said that Sikhs did not need another living Guru after him to teach them how to live their lives properly. He said the Guru Granth Sahib would be their guide after his death. This reminds Sikhs of the important teachings in the holy scripture.

▲ Guru Gobind Singh, the tenth Guru.

Guru Granth Sahib

manjii

offerings

Showing respect

When worshippers sit in the floor, they do not
point their feet at the Guru Granth Sahib as this
would be a sign of disrespect. The Guru Granth
Sahib is kept on a raised platform called a manjii so
everyone can see it.

▲ Worshippers bow to the
Guru Granth Sahib before
they sit down.

The Guru Granth Sahib

Sikhs think about the Guru Granth Sahib as being a religious teacher or Guru. The scripture contains the thoughts and writings of the Gurus that tells Sikhs how to lead a good life. The Guru Granth Sahib teaches Sikhs that they should be kind to everyone and that all people are equal and should be treated the same, no matter what their religion or beliefs. Hymns, or shabads (see pages 16-17), written by some of the Gurus are also part of the scripture. These are sung at all services and celebrations.

▲ The Guru Granth Sahib is written in the **Punjabi** language in a **script** called **Gurmukhi**.

▼ The first words of the Sikh holy scripture are, 'There is only one God'.

Covering the holy scripture

The Guru Granth Sahib is always covered by a cloth called a rumalla when it is not being read. Every night the holy scripture is put in a separate room to keep it safe and make sure it is not damaged.

Worship at home

Many Sikhs pray at home as well as in the gurdwara. They keep their own copy of the Guru Granth Sahib in a special place or room. They might visit it in the morning or at the end of the day. Members of the family can read from the scripture alone or together. While it is being read, Sikhs wave a fan called a chauri over the open Guru Granth Sahib. This is another sign of respect for the holy scripture.

▶ A chauri is waved over the Guru Granth Sahib as a sign of respect while it is being read.

chauri

A Sikh service

There is no special day for worship in the Sikh religion. A service is usually held on a Sunday for people who work during the week. When everyone is sitting down in the prayer hall, the Granthi opens the Guru Granth Sahib at any page and reads a verse from it. Other Sikhs who know and understand the language of the holy scripture may also read during the service.

▼ Sunday is a good day to worship for people who are busy during the rest of the week.

A Granthi reads from the Sikh Guru Granth Sahib during a service.

Granthi

There are no ministers or priests in the Sikh religion. Instead, every gurdwara has a Granthi. The word Granthi means 'reader of the Sikh scripture'. A Granthi's main duty is to read from the Guru Granth Sahib. The Granthi may also be responsible for looking after the gurdwara, and teaching and helping members of the Sikh community.

Leading prayers

The Granthi plans the services, leads prayers and makes sure the Guru Granth Sahib is put away each night. The Granthi must also be a member of the **Khalsa**.

THE KHALSA

When Sikhs are **baptised** they become members of the Khalsa. This means they will live by the teachings of the Gurus and keep the Five Ks (see pages 21–23). These teachings include never cutting their hair or taking drugs or alcohol. The Khalsa was founded in 1699 by Guru Gobind Singh. It started with five men who were willing to die for their faith. The five men are known as the Panj Pyare, or 'the five beloved ones'. Most Sikhs are baptised and join the Khalsa.

▲ Guru Gobind Singh with the five men who formed the first Khalsa.

prayers are led
by a Granthi

Saying prayers

Everyone stands up to say a prayer called the Ardas.
When Sikhs say this prayer they remember God,
the Gurus and all the people who have died for
Sikhism. They also ask for God's help and forgiveness.
Other prayers ask God to bless all people. Everyone says
'Waheguru,' which is Punjabi for 'praise be to God'.

Respect and help

During the service, the Granthi may also give a talk
about how to be a good Sikh. Young Sikhs are taught
to respect parents and elders. They are taught to
help their parents at home with housework and
with preparing meals.

▲ When Sikhs pray
they put their
hands together and
close their eyes.
This helps them to
think about what
they are doing.

Eating karah prashad

At the end of the service everyone sits down to have some karah prashad, which is a soft, sweet dough made from flour, sugar, water and butter. This is a very important part of the service because Sikhs believe that eating karah prashad together shows that they are equal members of God's family. Anyone can eat karah prashad, no matter what their religion or how rich or poor they are. This is to show that everyone is equal in the eyes of God.

WHAT DO YOU THINK?

How do the teachings of the Gurus affect the way Sikhs behave every day?

Why do you think sharing and being kind to people makes you feel good?

▲ Worshippers are given karah prashad. They must sit to eat it and everyone must take a share.

Hymns and music

The Guru Granth Sahib includes lots of hymns, or shabads, written by the Gurus. These are sung during the service. Musicians called ragis play during the singing. They sit on one side of the platform where the Guru Granth Sahib is kept, so they do not have to turn their backs to the holy scripture. Everyone sits to listen or join in with the singing.

▼ Like all worshippers at the gurdwara, the musicians sit on the floor to play their instruments.

Joyful hymns

Music and singing play an important part in Sikh worship. The hymns remind Sikhs that worshipping God is joyful and should make them happy. The hymns also remind Sikhs of the teachings of the Gurus and to open their hearts to the love of God.

Musical instruments

The main instruments played by musicians in the gurdwara are the harmonium and Indian drums called tabla. The harmonium is like a small piano but it can be carried from one place to another.

▲ The tabla is a pair of hand drums played during a Sikh service. One drum is bigger than the other so they make different sounds.

▲ The harmonium makes a sound similar to an accordion.

WHAT DO YOU THINK?

Why are hymns a good thing to have as part of a religious service?

What makes religious music different from other music?

The langar

All gurdwaras have a food hall, or langar, that is a kitchen and an eating area. After the service everyone goes to the langar to have a meal together. The meal is also called 'langar' and is cooked, served and cleaned away by helpers called sewadars. The helpers can be men, women and children. The langar is **vegetarian** and no eggs are used, so all visitors can eat it. Langar is served at least once a day, every day of the year.

▼ In the langar people sit in rows on the floor to eat their meal.

⊙ Sikhism/Gurdwaras/Inside a Gurdwara

Sharing work and food

Sharing and helping others is a big part of the Sikh religion. This is why the langar is so important. Langar means 'shared food'. People donate whatever they can to the langar – food, money, time, even pots and pans. The food is simple but healthy, such as a vegetable curry with freshly made bread called chapatti.

▼ In this gurdwara in India, 2,000 people come to enjoy the langar every half an hour.

WHAT DO YOU THINK?

Why do you think it is important that people share a meal together?

Why is it a good idea for a family to eat a meal together once a day?

Signs and symbols

Sikhs have many important signs, symbols and religious objects. The Khanda is the symbol shown on the Sikh flag. It reminds Sikhs that God is powerful and that He is always present. On the inside of the circle is a double-edged sword that shows Sikhs believe in only one God. The circle means that God is **eternal**: He has no beginning or end. The two crossed swords outside the circle stand for the power of the Sikh faith.

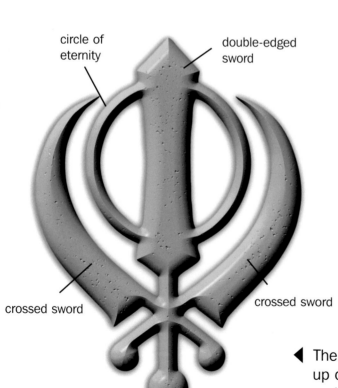

circle of eternity

double-edged sword

crossed sword

crossed sword

▲ The Nishan Sahib is the name of the orange flag that flies over every gurdwara. It has the Khanda symbol in the centre.

◀ The Khanda symbol is made up of a double-edged sword and two crossed swords.

⊙ Sikhism/Signs, Symbols and Religious Objects

The Five Ks

Sikh men and women who have been baptised wear five symbols that show they belong to the Khalsa. Each symbol begins with a 'K' in the Punjabi language, so the symbols are called the Five Ks.

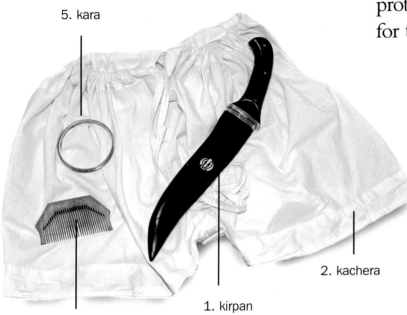

5. kara

4. kangha

1. kirpan

2. kachera

Kirpan

All Sikh men and women wear a short sword called a kirpan. The kirpan is not used as a weapon. It is a sign that Sikhs will always fight against evil, support truth and goodness, protect the weak, and stand up for their beliefs and their religion.

◀ Each of these items is a symbol for one of the Five Ks:
1. kirpan
2. kachera
3. kesh (see page 22)
4. kangha
5. kara (see page 23)

A SIKH BAPTISM

During baptism a bowl is filled with water and sugar. Prayers are said over the sweet water, called amrit, to make it holy. The person being baptised then drinks the water five times and has some sprinkled on his or her hair and eyes.

Kachera

Sikh men and women also wear special white cotton shorts called kachera. These are worn everyday under their clothes and for swimming or sports.

⊙ Sikhism/Signs, Symbols and Religious Objects

Kesh

Sikh men and women do not cut their hair, and men do not shave their beards. This is called kesh, or uncut hair. To keep their hair tidy, men tie it up in a turban. This is a sign of their religious identity. Young boys keep their hair neat in a cloth called a patka. Women can wear their hair loose or tied back, but all women wear a chunni, or scarf, to cover their hair when they enter the gurdwara.

▶ Sikh men tie a six-metre cloth around their head to make a turban. Women can also wear a turban but many wear a chunni.

Sikh men wear a turban to keep their hair tidy

Sikh women may cover their hair with a scarf

Kangha

Sikh men and women always carry a special wooden comb called a kangha. It is used to comb their hair, but it is also a reminder of cleanliness and the need to keep their lives in order.

Kara

The kara is a steel bangle that Sikh men and women wear on their right wrist. It is a sign that God has no beginning and no end.

▼ Young boys wear a kara on their right wrist when they have been baptised.

IK ONKAR

Ik Onkar means 'there is only one God', and these are the first words in the Guru Granth Sahib. The symbol for these words is often used as a decoration by Sikhs.

▲ The Ik Onkar symbol: Ik means 'one' and Onkar means 'God'.

kara

⊙ Sikhism/Signs, Symbols and Religious Objects

The Gurus

In the gurdwara there are often pictures of one or more of the ten Sikh Gurus who began the Sikh religion. These are only paintings and they are not worshipped. The Gurus taught that there is only one God, and that everyone is equal. They also taught that all people should be treated with kindness, no matter what their religion or background. The first Guru was **Guru Nanak** (1469-1539) and nine other Gurus followed him and added to the Sikh beliefs.

▶ Guru Nanak started Sikhism in India around CE 1500.

Writing the holy book

Guru Angad Dev (1504-52) was the second Guru. He collected the teachings of Guru Nanak and these, together with his own, are included in the Guru Granth Sahib. He developed a special script for writing the holy scripture called Gurmukhi, which means, 'the mouth of the Guru'.

A new gurdwara

Guru Ram Das (1534-81) built a holy city for Sikhs in India called Amritsar. Guru Arjan Dev (1563-1606) was the son of Guru Ram Das. He built the beautiful Harmandir Sahib (Golden Temple) on the side of a lake in Amritsar. The very first copy of the Guru Granth Sahib was placed in this gurdwara.

The last Guru

Guru Gobind Singh was the last Guru (1666-1708). He said there was no need for more human Gurus after him. He thought Sikhs should follow the teachings of the Guru Granth Sahib in the future.

▲ Guru Angad Dev wrote many holy poems praising God that are part of the Guru Granth Sahib.

HAR KRISHAN THE CHILD GURU

The youngest Guru was Har Krishan (1656–64). He became a Guru when he was just five years old. He caught **smallpox** and died when he was eight years old.

Sikh festivals

Sikhs have many festivals to remind them of special events in the history of their religion. One of the most important festivals is Baisakhi. This takes place in April and celebrates the time when Guru Gobind Singh gave Sikhs the Five Ks. It also happens at the same time as the **harvest festival**. It is a time of great joy with traditional Indian dancing and singing. During Baisakhi, Sikhs decorate their homes with flowers, visit the gurdwara and listen to readings from the Guru Granth Sahib.

▼ For the festival of Baisakhi, many Sikhs celebrate with colourful parades held near their gurdwara.

Lights and lanterns

The festival of lights, or Diwali, is when Sikhs celebrate the release of Guru Hargobind from the Muslims in 1619. They have a special service at the gurdwara and sing hymns and say prayers. It is a very happy time when families give each other sweets and watch fireworks.

▲ At Diwali, Sikhs light lanterns and candles at home and in the gurdwara.

Celebrating the Gurus

During festivals called gurpurbs, Sikhs remember the lives of the Gurus. Two of the most important gurpurbs celebrate the birthdays of Guru Nanak and Guru Gobind Singh. Sikhs decorate their gurdwara with flowers and flags, and in some places there are parades through the streets with singing and dancing.

▼ During a procession in India to celebrate Guru Nanak's birthday, Sikhs perform Gatka, a type of **martial art**.

GURPURB FESTIVALS

Gurpurb festivals begin at the gurdwara where several Sikhs take turns to read the Guru Granth Sahib non-stop from beginning to end. This can take about 48 hours.

Holy places

One of the most important holy places for Sikhs is the Harmandir Sahib, or Golden Temple. This is in the city of Amritsar in the Punjab, north-west India. The name Harmandir Sahib means 'God's place'. Sikhs go to the Golden Temple to strengthen their belief in God and the teachings of the Gurus. Visitors sometimes bathe in the lake surrounding the temple while listening to hymns. Next to the Harmandir Sahib, there are two huge langar halls and **dormitories** where visitors can eat and sleep free of charge.

▼ Thousands of visitors from around the world go to the Harmandir Sahib to worship.

House of Guru Nanak

Another historic place for Sikhs is the house where Guru Nanak was born, outside the city of Lahore in Pakistan. Guru Nanak spent most of his life travelling around India, **meditating** and spreading the message of Sikhism.

▲ Part of the house where Guru Nanak was born is now a gurdwara called Nankana Sahib.

House of Guru Gobind Singh

For nearly 25 years, Guru Gobind Singh lived in the city of Anandpur in India. The Anandpur Sahib gurdwara is built on the place where he started the Khalsa (see page 13).

▼ The Anandpur Sahib gurdwara is in Anandpur, which is known as the 'Holy City of Bliss'.

Glossary

baptism   a ceremony in which someone joins the Sikh religion

canopy   a cloth covering held up at each corner by four poles

donation   any item that is given as a gift to help a good cause

dormitories   rooms where lots of people sleep

eternal   for ever

Gurmukhi script   a type of writing used for the Sikh holy scripture, the Guru Granth Sahib

Guru   a Sikh teacher. The Sikh faith is based on the teaching and writings of ten Gurus

Guru Granth Sahib   the Sikh holy scripture

Guru Nanak   the first Sikh Guru, who started the Sikh religion

harvest festival   a celebration to thank God for a good harvest

Khalsa   full members of the Sikh religion, who have been baptised and who wear the Five Ks

martial art   a way of defending yourself if you are attacked

meditate   to sit quietly and empty your mind so that you feel calm and relaxed

Punjabi   the language spoken in a part of India called the Punjab

respect   to show how much you value someone or something; to treat with care

Sikh   the word Sikh means 'a learner or follower'. It is used to describe a person who believes in Sikhism

smallpox   an illness that can kill young children unless they are vaccinated against it

vegetarian   someone who does not eat meat or fish

Quizzes

Try these questions to see how much you remember about Sikhism.

Are these facts true or false?

1. A gurdwara is a place where Sikhs worship.

2. The langar is where Sikhs pray.

3. The Guru Granth Sahib is the name of the Sikh holy scripture.

4. Sikhs wear turbans to keep warm.

5. Sikhs believe that 12 Gurus began the Sikh religion.

Below are four of the Five Ks. Match the name to the object.

a. kirpan

b. kara

c. kangha

d. kachera

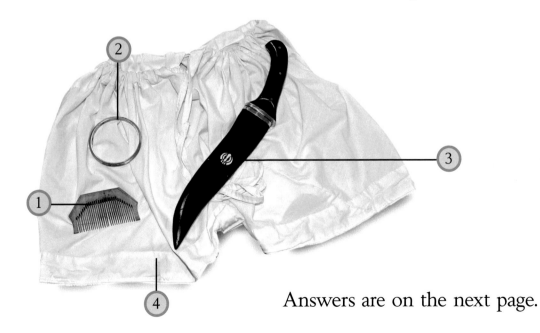

Answers are on the next page.

Index

Answers

1 True
2 False, the langar is a shared vegetarian meal and name for a food hall.
3 True
4 False, Sikhs wear turbans as part of their religious identity.
5 False, ten Gurus founded the Sikh religion.

Match the name to the object: a3; b2; c1; d4.

OUR PLACES OF WORSHIP

Contents of titles in the series:

WAYLAND